CONTENTS

Q & A

Jokes

Q: What's the difference between a guitar and a fish?

A: You can't tuna fish.

Q: What did 0 say to 8?

A: Nice belt!

Q: What do kids play when they can't play with a phone?

A: Bored games.

Q: How do billboards talk?

A: Sign language.

Q: Why was the broom late for school?

A: It overswept!

Q: Why did the computer go to the doctor?

A: It had a blue tooth.

Q: Why are pirates called pirates?

A: Because they aaarrreee?

Q: What did one plate say to the other plate?

A: He said, "Lunch is on me!"

Q: Why do birds fly to warmer climates in the winter?

A: It's much easier than walking!

Q: Why did the superhero flush the toilet?

A: Because it was his doody.

Q: If you are American in the living room, what are you in the bathroom?

A: Euro-peein'

Q: What game does the sky love to play?

A: Twister

3

Q: Did you hear the joke about the roof?

A: Never mind, it's over your head.

Q: Did you hear the joke about the little mountain?

A: Ya, it's hill-arious!

Q: How do you get a tissue to dance?

A: You put a little boogie in it.

Q: What's brown and sticky?

A: A stick

Q: What do you call an alligator in a vest?

A: An investigator.

Q: What do you call a fake noodle?

A: An im-pasta.

Q: Why did the banana go to the hospital?

A: He was peeling really bad.

Q: Why did the tomato blush?

A: Because he saw the salad dressing.

Q: What does the cloud wear under his raincoat?

A: Thunderwear.

Q: Why are teddy bears never hungry?

A: They're always stuffed!

Q: How do vampires start their letter?

A: "Tomb it may concern..."

Q: What is Fast Food?

A: A chicken running down the road.

Q: What room can no one enter?

A: A mush-room.

Q: How do all the oceans say hello to each other?

A: They wave!

Q: What do you call an old snowman?

A: Water.

Q: What has four wheels and flies?

A: A garbage truck.

Q: What do you call a train that sneezes?

A: Achoo-choo train.

Q: What is the best cure for dandruff?

A: Baldness.

Q: Why do graveyards have a fence around them?

A: Because people are dying to get in.

Q: What do lawyers wear to court?

A: Lawsuits!

Q: What did the policeman say to his tummy?

A: You're under a vest!

Q: What is a pencil's favorite place to go on vacation?

A: Pencil-vania!

Q: What did one eye say to the other eye?

A: Between you and me something smells.

Q: What can you catch from a vampire in winter-time?

A: Frost-bite!

Q: Why do bees have sticky hair?

A: They use a honey comb.

Q: What has hundreds of ears but can't hear a thing?

A: A cornfield.

Q: Where do crayons go on vacation?

A: Color-ado!

Q: Why was the picture sent to jail?

A: It was framed!

Q: Which superhero hits the most home runs?

A: Batman.

Q: How do you catch a whole school of fish?

A: With bookworms.

Q: Why didn't the zombie go to school?

A: He felt rotten!

Q: Why is a baseball
stadium always cool?

A: It is full of fans.

Q: Why do dragons
sleep during the day?

A: So they can
fight knights!

Q: What did Bacon
say to Tomato?

A: Lettuce get together!

Q: What do you call
a computer the sings?

A: A-Dell.

Q: What are the strongest
days of the week?

A: Saturday and Sunday.
All the others are weekdays.

Q: What did one tonsil
say to the other?

A: Better get dressed.
The doc's taking us out
tonight!

Q: What do Italian
ghosts have for dinner?

A: Spook-hetti!

Q: How much does a
pirate pay for corn?

A: A BUCK-aneer.

Q: Why couldn't the
pirate learn the alphabet?

A: Because he was
always lost at C.

Q: What is heavy forward
but not backward?

A: Ton

Q: What runs but
never walks?

A: Water!

Q: What's orange and sounds like a parrot?

A: A carrot!

Q: What do you call guy lying on your doorstep?

A: Matt.

Q: Why can't you ever tell a joke around glass?

A: It could crack up.

Q: Why is a cemetery a great place to write a story?

A: Because there are so many plots there!

Q: What did the man say when he walked into a bar?

A: Ouch!

Q: How do you talk to giants?

A: Use big words!

Q: What do you get if you cross a cat with a dark horse?

A: Kitty Perry.

Q: Why couldn't the teddy bear finish dinner?

A: He was stuffed.

Q: What do snowmen call their fancy annual dance?

A: The Snowball.

Q: How do you know when a bike is thinking?

A: You can see its wheel turning.

Q: What do female ghosts use to do their makeup?

A: Vanishing Cream!

Q: What do you call a three-footed AARDVARK?

A: YARDVARK!.

Q: What's the best thing about Switzerland?

A: I don't know, but the flag is a big plus.

Q: How did the farmer fix his jeans?

A: With a cabbage patch!

Q: What do you do if you see a spaceman?

A: Park your car, man.

Q: How did the baby tell her mom that she had a wet diaper?

A: She sent her a pee-mail.

Q: How did Benjamin Franklin feel when he discovered electricity?

A: Shocked!

Q: What do witches ask for at hotels?

A: Broom service!

Q: What did the inventor of the door-knocker win?

A: The no-bell prize.

Q: What do you call a boomerang that won't come back?

A: A stick.

Q: What washes up on really small beaches?

A: Micro-waves.

Tongue twister:

Selfish shellfish.
(say it 10 times)

9

Q: Why did the cookie go to the hospital?

A: Because he was feeling crummy.

Q: What kind of shoes do private investigators wear?

A: Sneak-ers.

Q: What do ghosts wear when their eyesight gets blurred?

A: Spooktacles.

Q: Why do shoemakers go to heaven?

A: Because they have good soles.

Q: Who earns a living driving their customers away?

A: A taxi driver.

Q: Why was the sand wet?

A: Because the sea weed.

Q: Why do we never tell jokes about pizza?

A: They're too cheesy.

Q: What stays in the corner yet travels all over the world?

A: A stamp.

Q: Why did the golfer wear two pairs of pants?

A: In case he got a hole in one.

Q: What would be the national holiday for a nation of vampires?

A: Fangs-giving!

Q: What do you call cheese that's not your cheese?

A: Nacho cheese.

Q: Why did they bury the battery?

A: Because it was dead.

Q: What's Irish and stays out all night long?

A: Pati'o furniture.

Q: What do you call a laughing jar of mayonnaise?

A: LMAYO

Q: Did you hear the joke about the roof?

A: Never mind, it's over your head.

Q: What is a skeleton's favorite musical instrument?

A: A trombone!

Q: What kind of music do mummies listen to?

A: Wrap music.

Q: Did you hear about the population of Ireland?

A: It's Dublin.

Q: Why were the ink spots crying?

A: Because their mother was in the pen and they didn't know how long the sentence would be.

Q: How do you make an artichoke?

A: You strangle it.

Q: What did the fireman name his twin sons?

A: Jose and Hose-B.

Q: What time is it when people are throwing pieces of bread at you?

A: Time to duck.

Q: How many apples grow on a tree?

A: All of them.

Q: What does a ghost call his mom and dad?

A: His trans-parents.

Q: What type of jokes do you make in the shower?

A: Clean jokes!

Q: Why are all of Superman's costumes tight?

A: They're all size S.

Q: What has one eye but cannot see?

A: A needle.

Q: Why did Humpty Dumpty have a great fall?

A: To make up for his miserable summer.

Q: What do you do if someone rolls their eyes at you?

A: Roll them back.

Q: How do you get inside a locked cemetery?

A: Use a Skeleton Key to unlock the gates!

Q: Why did the girl throw a stick of butter?

A: She wanted to see a butter fly.

Q: What did the baby corn say to the mama corn?

A: Where's Popcorn?

Q: How many lips does a flower have?

A: Tu-lips.

Q: Why was the skeleton afraid of the storm?

A: He didn't have any guts.

Q: What did the sink say to the potty?

A: You look flushed!

Q: What is the name of the witch who lives in the desert?

A: Sand-witch!

Q: What do you call a sad coffee?

A: Despresso.

13

Q: Why is England
the wettest country?

A: Because the queen
has reigned there
for years!

Q: Why did the skeleton
climb up the tree?

A: Because a dog was
after his bones!

Q: Do you know how
many famous men and
women were born on
your birthday?

A: None, only babies.

Q: What word starts
with E, ends with E, but
has only one letter in it?

A: Envelope.

Q: What did the finger
say to the thumb?

A: I'm in glove with you.

Q: What do elves
do after school?

A: Their gnome work.

Q: Why did the
man put his money
in the freezer?

A: He wanted cold,
hard cash.

Q: Why did the computer
go to the doctor?

A: Because it had a virus!

Q: Why did the God
of Thunder need to
stretch his muscles
son much when he
was a kid?

A: He was a little Thor.

Q: Which hand is better to write with?

A: Neither, it's better to write with a pen.

Q: Did you hear about the cheese factory that exploded in France?

A: There was nothing left but de Brie.

Q: Where do ghosts like to travel on vacation?

A: The Dead Sea!

Q: Why did the boy bring a ladder to school?

A: Because he wanted to go to high school.

Q: Should you have your whole family for Thanksgiving dinner?

A: No, you should just stick with turkey.

Q: How do you make holy water?

A: You boil the hell out of it!

Q: What nails do carpenters hate hammering?

A: Fingernails.

Q: Dad, did you get a haircut?

A: No. I got them all cut.

Q: What do you call a smart group of trees?

A: A brainforest.

Q: What kind of nut doesn't like money?

A: Cash-eww.

Q: What do ghosts use to wash their hair?

A: Sham-BOO!

Q: Want to hear a joke about paper?

A: Never mind, it's tearable (terrible!).

Q: Why was the burglar so sensitive?

A: He takes things personally.

Q: What did the digital clock say to the grandfather clock?

A: Look, Grandpa! No hands!

Q: Why did the bicycle fall over?

A: It was two tired.

Q: How do you define a good farmer?

A: A man who is outstanding in his field.

Q: What do you call a man with no body and just a nose?

A: Nobody nose.

Q: Why did the coffee file a police report?

A: It got mugged.

Q: How to mountains stay warm in winter?

A: Snowcaps.

Q: Why didn't the skeleton like to talk on the rotary skelephone?

A: Because he preferred his cell bone.

Q: Why didn't the
lamp sink?

A: Because it was
too light.

Q: How did the skeleton
know it was going to
rain on Halloween?

A: He could feel
it in his bones!

Q: What does a clock
do when it's hungry?

A: Goes back 4 seconds!

Q: What do you call
a guy with a rubber toe?

A: Roberto.

Q: Why do vampires
seem sick?

A: They're always coffin.

Q: Why did the man
run around his bed?

A: He was trying to
catch up on sleep!

Q: Who helps little
pumpkins cross the road
on the way to school?

A: The Crossing Gourd!

Q: Why is DARK spelled
with a K not a C?

A: Because you can't
see in the dark.

Q: Can February March?

A: No, but April May.

Q: Why did the scarecrow win an award?

A: Because he was outstanding in his field.

Q: Why shouldn't you tell secrets in a cornfield?

A: There are too many ears.

Q: What do you call a nosy pepper?

A: Jalapeno business!

Q: Why did Mickey Mouse become an astronaut?

A. So he could visit Pluto!

Q: Why did the student eat his homework?

A: Because the teacher told him it was a piece of cake!

Q: Why did the kid throw the clock out the window?

A: He wanted to see time fly.

Q: What happened to the skeleton who stayed by the fire for too long?

A: He became bone dry.

Q: What did the mayo say when the refrigerator door opened?

A: "Close the door! I'm dressing!"

18

Q: Want to hear a joke about construction?

A: Actually, I'm still working on it.

Q: Why couldn't Dracula's wife fall asleep?

A: Because of his coffin!

Q: Why did the kid cross the playground?

A: To get to the other slide.

Q: What did the snowman ask the other snowman?

A: Do you smell carrots?

Q: Why shouldn't you give Elsa a balloon?

A. Because she'll let it go!

Q. What does the ghost call his true love?

A. My ghoul-friend.

Tongue Twister:
I saw a kitten eating chicken in the kitchen.

Q: What kind of tree can fit into your hand?

A: A palm tree!

Q: What is brown and has a head and a tail but no legs?

A: A penny.

Q: What did the grape do when he got stepped on?

A: He let out a little wine.

Q: Did I tell you the time I fell in love during a backflip?

A: I was head over heels.

Q: What do you call a guy who never farts in public?

A: A private tutor.

19

Q: What did the big flower say to the little flower?

A: Hi, bud!

Q: What happens if you eat too many Christmas decorations?

A: You get "Tinsel"-itis!

Q: Why did the can-crusher quit his job?

A: Because it was soda-pressing.

Q: How can you tell that a tree is a dogwood tree?

A: By its bark!

Q: What did the fisherman say to the magician?

A: Pick a cod, any cod.

Q: What is the tallest building in the world?

A: The library! It has the most stories!

Q. How did the phone propose to his girlfriend on Valentine's Day?

A. He gave her a ring.

Q: Why are skeletons so good at chopping down trees?

A: They're LUMBARjacks!

Q: Did you hear about the kid-napping at school?

A: It's fine, he woke up.

Q: Why did the skeleton go to the dance alone?

A: He had no body to go with him!

Q: What is the best day to
go to the beach?

A: Sunday, of course!

Q: Why do we tell actors to break a leg?

A: Because every play has a cast.

Q: Why shouldn't you play cards in the jungle?

A: There are too many cheetahs!

Q: What makes the calendar look so popular?

A: It has so many dates!

Q: What sits at the bottom of the sea and twitches?

A: A nervous wreck.

Q: What do Olympic sprinters eat before a race?

A: Nothing. They fast.

Q: What did the limestone say to the geologist?

A: Please don't take me for granite.

Q. What did the little boat say to the yacht?

A. Can I interest you in a little row-mance?

Q: What did the stamp say to the envelope?

A: Stick with me and we'll go places together.

Q: What's the first bet that most people make in their lives?

A: The Alpha-bet.

Q: Why do bowling pins have such a hard life?

A: They're always getting knocked down.

Q: Why are skeletons
so calm?

A: Because nothing
gets under their skin!

Q: Why wouldn't the
teacher bring the class
to the pumpkin patch?

A: It was in a seedy
part of town.

Q: Why didn't the
baby skeleton cross
the road alone?

A: Because his mummy
was not there!

Q: How do you organize
a space party?

A: You planet!

Q: What kind of
button can't be bought
from a tailor?

A: A belly button!

Q: What do ghosts
like to drink the most?

A: Ghoul-ade!

Q: What did the paper
say to the pencil?

A: Write on!

Q: Where were
pencils invented?

A: PENCIL-vania.

Q: Is this pool safe
for diving?

A: It deep ends.

Tongue Twisters:

Blake's black bike's back
brake bracket block broke.

Q: Why does bees hum?

A: Because they don't know the words.

Q: What do you call security guards working outside Samsung shops?

A: Guardians of the Galaxy.

Q: What did the scarf say to the hat?

A: "I'll hang around, you go on a-head!"

Q: What time is it when you have to go to the dentist?

A: Tooth-hurty!

Q: Where do hamburgers go dancing?

A: A meatball.

Q: Where do you learn to make ice cream?

A: Sundae school.

Q: Who was the most famous skeleton detective?

A: Sherlock Bones.

Q: What do you call having your grandma on speed dial?

A: Instagram.

Q: What did one elevator say to the other elevator?

A: I think I'm coming down with something!

Q: What did Jack say to Jill after they rolled down the hill?

A: I think I spilled the water.

Q: What's red and bad for your teeth?

A: Brick.

Q: What does the skeleton chef say when he serves you a meal?

A: "Bone Appetit!"

Q: What happened to the pirate ship that sank in the sea full of sharks?

A: It came back with a skeleton crew!

Q: Why did Charlie go out with a prune?

A: Because he couldn't find a date!

Q: What did the officer molecule say to the suspect molecule?

A: I've got my ion you.

Q: What are bald sea captains most worried about?

A: Cap sizes.

Q: What did one thirsty vampire say to the other as they were passing the morgue?

A: Let's stop in for a cool one!

Q: How can you tell if a vampire has a horrible cold?

A: By his deep loud coffin!

Q: What kind of car does Mickey Mouse's wife drive?

A: A minnie van, of course.

Q: What do you call a retired vegetable?

A: A has-bean.

Q: Why did the vampire get fired from the blood bank?

A: He was caught drinking on the job!

Q: What's blue and smells like red paint?

A: Blue paint.

Q: How do elves learn how to spell?

A: They study the elf-abet.

Q: Why didn't the skeleton want to go to school?

A: His heart wasn't in it.

Q: What kind of monster loves to disco?

A: The boogieman.

Q: When is the moon heaviest?

A: When it's full.

Q: Who can shave six times a day, but still have a beard?

A: A barber.

Q: What is a witch's favorite subject in school?

A: Spelling!

Q: What's it called when a vampire has trouble with his house?

A: A grave problem.

Q: What does Christmas have to do with a cat lost in the desert?

A: They both have sandy claws.

Q: What crime is an egg most afraid of?

A: Poaching!

Q: Why was the baby strawberry crying?

A: Because her parents were in a jam.

Q: Why were bikes suspended from school?

A: They spoke too much.

Q: What kind of music do balloons hate?

A: Pop.

Q: What's it like to be kissed by a vampire?

A: It's a pain in the neck.

Q: What is in a ghost's nose?

A: Boo-gers.

Q: Why don't mummies take time off?

A: They're afraid to unwind.

Q: Why did the boy do homework on a plane?

A: He wanted a higher education.

Q: What bow can't be tied?

A: A rainbow!

Q: Why are horses such lousy dancers?

A: They have two left feet!

Q: What do you call a laughing motorcycle?

A: A Yamahahaha.

Q: Why did the bubblegum cross the road?

A: Because it was stuck to the chicken's foot.

Q: What time is it when a ball goes through the window?

A: Time to get a new window.

Q: What did the traffic light say to the car?

A: Don't look. I'm about to change.

Q: Why did the headless horseman go into business?

A: He wanted to get ahead in life.

Tongue Twisters:

Six sick hicks nick six slick bricks with picks and sticks.

28

Q: Why did the Vampire read the New York Times?

A: He heard it had great circulation.

Q: How much does it cost a pirate to get his ears pierced?

A: About a buck an ear.

Q: Did you hear about the two guys who stole a calendar?

A: They each got six months.

Q: Where did the computer go to dance?

A: To a disc-o.

Q: What does a meditating egg say?

A: Ohhhhhmmmlet!

Q: How can you make seven even?

A: Take away the S.

Q: Why are pianos hard to open?

A: The keys are inside.

Q: What do you call a sad strawberry?

A: A blueberry.

Q: What has one head, one foot and four legs?

A: A Bed.

Q: What do you always get on your birthday?

A: Another year older!

Q: How does a cucumber become a pickle?

A: It goes through a jarring experience.

Q: What do snowmen like to do on the weekend?

A: Chill out.

Q: What does Jack Frost like best about school?

A: Snow and tell.

Q: What did one flag say to the other flag?

A: Nothing. It just waved!

Q: How do you know if your clock is crazy?

A: It goes "cuckoo!"

Q: Don't leave any food around your computer.

A: It takes a lot of bytes.

Q: What nationality is Santa Claus?

A: North Polish.

Q: What's a king's favorite kind of weather?

A: Reign.

Q: Does a pink candle burn longer than a blue one?

A: No, they both burn shorter!

Q: Why do we put candles on the top of birthday cakes?

A: Because it's too hard to put them on the bottom!

Q: What did the broccoli say to the celery?

A: Quit stalking me.

Q: What sort of birthday cake do ghosts prefer?

A: An "I scream" cake.

Q: What is the difference between a school teacher and a train?

A: The teacher says spit your gum out and the train says "chew chew chew".

Q: What do you get if you cross an iPad with a Christmas tree?

A: A pineapple!

Q: What has a jolly laugh, brings you presents and scratches up your furniture?

A: Santa Claws.

Q: What do road crews use at the North Pole?

A: Snow cones!

Q: What day of the week
do eggs hate?

A: Fry-day!

Q: What did the nose
say to the finger?

A: Quit picking on me!

Q: What did Aquaman
say to his kids when they
wouldn't eat their food?

A: Water you waiting for?

Q: How do you take
your coffee?

A: Very, very seriously.

Q: What do you call
sad coffee?

A: Despresso.

Q: Why did the
cross-eyed teacher
lose her job?

A: Because she
couldn't control
her pupils?

Q: What is black and
white and sleeps a lot?

A: A snoozepaper!

Hilarious Animal Jokes

What do you call a
sheep with no legs?

A cloud.

What do sharks
say when something
cool happens?

Jawesome!

How do you spot
a modern spider?

He doesn't have a
web, he has a website!

What creature is smarter
than a talking parrot?

A spelling bee.

What do pigs put
on sore toes?

Oinkment!

What do you get
when you cross a snake
and a kangaroo?

A jump rope.

What does a clam
do on his birthday?

He shellabrates!

What did the porcupine
say to the cactus?

Is that you, Mama?

Two fish are sitting in
a tank. One looks over
at the other and says:
"Hey, do you know how
to drive this thing?"

How does a hen
leave the house?

Through the egg-sit!

34

What do you call a
bear with no teeth?

A Gummy Bear.

What do you call a
pig that knows karate?

A pork chop.

What's the difference
between a fly and a bird?

A bird can fly but
a fly can't bird!

Where's the best place
to get information
about eggs?

The hen-cyclopedia!

What kind of bird is
always depressed?

Blue jays.

What do you call
a bee that lives
in America?

USB

What do you say
to a kangaroo on
its birthday?

Hoppy Birthday!

Why are fish so smart?

Because they live in schools.

What do cows read?

Cattle-logs.

What sound do porcupines
make when they kiss?

Ouch!

Why did Mozart
sell his chickens?

They kept saying,
"Bach, Bach, Bach."

What do you give
a sick bird?

A special tweetment.

What do sheep do
on sunny days?

Have a baa – baa – cue!

What animal can you
always find at a
baseball game?

A bat.

What do camels have
that no other animal has?

Baby camels.

Where do horses live?

In neiiiiigh-borhoods!

What's worse than
raining cats and dogs?

Hailing taxis!

How do porcupines
play leapfrog?

Very carefully!

Why does a chicken
coop have two doors?

If it had four, it would
be a chicken sedan.

Why do cows use
the doorbell?

Because their horns
don't work!

Why did the lion
eat a light bulb?

He wanted a light lunch.

What do you call a seagull
when it flies over a bay?

A bagel.

**What do you call
two birds in love?**

Tweet-hearts!

**Why did the turkey
cross the road?**

It was the chicken's
day off!

**What do you call
a fish with no eye?**

Fsh.

**What do you call a
monster with no neck?**

The Lost Neck Monster.

**How does a penguin
build its house?**

Igloos it together.

**Why did the giraffe
get bad grades?**

Because he had his
head in the clouds.

**Why do fish live
in salt water?**

Because pepper makes
them sneeze!

**What's the
difference between
a guitar and a fish?**

You can tune a guitar
but you can't tunafish.

**What do fish sing
during winter?**

Christmas corals.

**Why did King Kong
climb the Empire
State Building?**

He couldn't fit
in the elevator.

**What time do
ducks wake up?**

At the quack of dawn!

What do you call a
shark that delivers
toys at Christmas?

Santa Jaws!

What animal dresses
up and howls?

A wearwolf.

Why are penguins
socially awkward?

Because they can't
break the ice.

Why are frogs
so happy?

They eat whatever
bugs them.

What does a
spider's bride wear?

A webbing dress.

Which subject does
a snake love most?

Hiss-tory.

What do you call a
duck that gets all A's?

A wise quacker.

Why do seagulls
live by the sea?

Because if they
lived by the bay,
they'd be bagels!

Why couldn't the
duck pay for dinner?

Her bill was too big.

What do you call
a dinosaur with an
extensive vocabulary?

A thesaurus.

What do you call an elephant in a phone booth?

Stuck!

I just watched a program about beavers. It was the best DAM program I've evet seen.

What does a panda ghost eat?

Bam-BOO!

Why can't you hear a pterodactyl go to the bathroom?

Because the pee is silent.

Why can't you trust the king of the jungle?

Because he is always lion.

What do you get when you cross a fish and an elephant?

Swimming trunks.

What's the difference between an elephant and a flea?

An elephant can have fleas but a flea can't have elephants.

What do birds say on Halloween to get candy?

Twick-or-tweet.

What's the difference between a BMW and a porcupine?

One has its pricks on the outside.

Two tigers were eating a clown. What did one of the tigers say to the other?

"Does this taste funny to you?"

When is it bad luck to be followed by a black cat?

When you're a mouse.

Why did the chicken
cross the road?
To get The Chinese Daily.
Do you get it?
No
Me neither. I get
The Times.

Where do cows go
on December 31st?

A moo year's eve party.

What happened
to the dog that
swallowed a firefly?

It barked with de-light.

What are caterpillars
scared of?

Dog-erpillars!

Why don't dinosaurs
eat clowns?

Because they
taste funny.

What do you call a
monkey that loves
potato chips?

A chipmunk.

Why did daddy rabbit
go to the barber?

Because he had a
lot of little hares.

Why can't you
trust zookeepers?

They love cheetahs.

Have you heard about
the pregnant bed bug?

She's going to have
her baby in the spring.

How do you make
an octopus laugh?

With ten-tickles.

Where do bees go
to the bathroom?

At the BP station!

What time is it
when an elephant
sits on your fence?

Time to get
a new fence.

What did the
duck say when he
bought lipstick?

Put it on my bill.

What do birds give
out on Halloween?

Tweets.

What do you get
when you cross a parrot
and a centipede?

A walkie-talkie!

Why should you
never trust a pig
with a secret?

Because it is
bound to squeal.

Why did they stop
giving tests at the zoo?

Because it was
full of cheetahs.

What key can never
unlock a door?

A monkey.

What does a
cow do for fun?

Goes to the moo-vies.

Tongue Twister:
I wish to wish the
wish you wish to wish,
but if you wish the
wish the witch wishes,
I won't wish the wish
you wish to wish.

What do you call
a dinosaur that
crashes his car?

Tyrannosaurus Wrecks.

What do you call a
donkey with three legs?

A Wonkey.

What kind of fish does
NASA send to space?

A bass-tronaut!

Why do giraffes have
such long necks?

Because they have
smelly feet.

What do you call
a sleeping bull?

A bulldozer!

Where do polar bears
keep their money?

In a snow bank!

What do you call
a pile of kittens?

A meow-ntain.

What did the
mother elephant say
to her kids when they
weren't behaving?

Tusk, tusk.

Why did the dinosaur cross the road?

Because chicken's didn't exist yet!

What do you call a pig that knows karate?

Pork Chop.

What did the buffalo say to his kid when he dropped him off for school?

Bi-son.

What do you get when you cross an elephant and a potato?

Mashed potatoes.

What dog would Dracula love to have as a pet?

Blood hound!

What makes more noise than a cat meowing outside your window?

Seven cats meowing outside your window.

How do you shoot a killer bee?

With a bee bee gun.

What do you call a blind dinosaur?

A do-you-think-he-saw-us.

What event do spiders love to attend?

Webbings.

Why do ducks have tail feathers?

To cover their buttquacks.

Where do you find
a dog with no legs?

Where you left him.

What do you call
a magic dog?

A Labracadabrador.

Knock-
Knock
Jokes

Knock, knock.
Who's there?
Who.
Who who?
Hold on. Is there
an owl in here?

Knock, knock.
Who's there?
Beets!
Beets who?
Beets me!

Knock, knock.
Who's there?
Nana.
Nana who?
Nana your business
who's there.

Knock, knock.
Who's there?
Donut.
Donut who?
Donut ask,
it's a secret!

Knock, knock.
Who's there?
Atch.
Atch who?
God bless you!

Knock, knock.
Who's there?
A broken pencil.
Broken pencil who?
Never mind,
it's pointless.

Knock, knock.
Who's there?
Honey bee.
Honey bee who?
Honey, be a
dear and make
me a sandwich!

Knock, knock.
Who's there?
Ice cream.
Ice cream who?
Ice cream if you
don't let me inside!

Knock, knock.
Who's there?
Cash.
Cash who?
Thanks, but
I would rather
have some
peanuts.

Knock, knock.
Who's there?
Yacht.
Yacht who?
Yacht a know
me by now!

Knock, knock.
Who's there?
Boo.
Boo who?
Don't cry,
it's just me.

Knock, knock.
Who's there?
A little old lady.
A little old lady who?
I didn't know that
you could yodel.

Knock, knock.
Who's there?
Banana.
Banana who?
Banana split!

Knock, knock.
Who's there?
Iva.
Iva who?
Iva sore hand
from knocking.

Knock, knock.
Who's there?
Beef.
Beef who?
Before I get
cold, you'd
better let me in!

Knock, knock.
Who's there?
Butter.
Butter who?
Butter be quick.
I have to go to
the bathroom!

Knock, knock.
Who's there?
Figs.
Figs who?
Figs the doorbell,
it is broken!

Knock, knock.
Who's there?
Leaf.
Leaf who?
Leaf me alone.

Knock, knock.
Who's there?
Abe.
Abe who?
Abe C D E F G H ...

Knock, knock.
Who's there?
Stopwatch.
Stopwatch who?
Stopwatch you're doing
and open the door!

Knock, knock.
Who's there?
Kiwi.
Kiwi who?
Kiwi go to the store?

Knock, knock.
Who's there?
Cow says.
Cow says who?
NOOOOOOO!
A cow says moo!

Did you hear about
the guy who invented
the knock-knock joke?
He won the
'No-Bell' prize.

Knock, knock.
Who's there?
Thermos.
Thermos who?
Thermos be a
better knock knock
joke than this!

Knock, knock.
Who's there?
Lettuce.
Lettuce who?
Lettuce in. we're
cold out here!

Knock, knock.
Who's there?
Ice cream soda.
Ice cream soda who?
Ice cream soda
people can hear me!

Knock, knock.
Who's there?
Ketchup.
Ketchup who?
Ketchup with me
and I'll tell you!

Knock, knock.
Who's there?
Isma.
Isma who?
Isma dinner ready yet?

Knock, knock.
Who's there?
Ida.
Ida who?
Ida know, you tell me.

Knock, knock.
Who's there?
Olive.
Olive who?
Olive right next
door to you.

Knock, knock.
Who's there?
Olive.
Olive who?
Olive you. Do you
love me too?

Knock, knock.
Who's there?
Water.
Water who?
Water way to
answer the door.

Knock, knock.
Who's there?
Pecan.
Pecan who?
Pecan someone
your own size?

Knock, knock.
Who's there?
Abby.
Abby who?
Abby birthday to you!

Knock, knock.
Who's there?
Orange.
Orange who?
Orange you going
to answer the door?

Knock, knock.
Who's there?
Orange.
Orange who?
Orange you glad
to see me?

Knock, knock.
Who's there?
Ada.
Ada who?
Ada burger for lunch!

Knock, knock.
Who's there?
Turnip.
Turnip who?
Turnip the volume,
it's quiet in here.

49

Knock, knock.
Who's there?
Butter.
Butter who?
It is butter if
you don't know.

Knock, knock.
Who's there?
Mikey.
Mikey who?
Mikey won't unlock
this door, so let me in!

Knock, knock.
Who's there?
Banana.
Banana who?
Knock, knock.
Who's there?
Banana.
Banana who?
Knock, knock.
Who's there?
Orange.
Orange who?
Orange you
glad I didn't
say banana
again?!?

Knock, knock.
Who's there?
Murry.
Murry who?
Murry Christmas,
one and all!

Knock, knock.
Who's there?
Cargo.
Cargo who?
Gar go "beep beep.
Vroom, vroom!"!

Knock, knock.
Who's there?
Lion.
Lion who?
Lion on your
doorstep- open up!

Knock, knock.
Who's there?
Barbie.
Barbie who?
Barbie Q Chicken!

Knock, knock.
Who's there?
Alex.
Alex who?
Alexi-plain when
you open the door!

Knock, knock.
Who's there?
Alfie.
Alfie who?
Alfie terrible
if you leave!

Knock, knock.
Who's there?
Yule log.
Yule log who?
Yule log the door
after you let me
in, won't you?

Knock, knock.
Who's there?
Ken.
Ken who?
Ken I come in,
it's freezing
out here?

Knock, knock.
Who's there?
Billy Bob Joe
Penny.
Billy Bob Joe
Penny who?
Exactly how
many Billy Bob
Joe ennies do
you know?

Knock, knock.
Who's there?
Bless!
Bless who?
I didn't sneeze!

Knock, knock.
Who's there?
Radio.
Radio who?
Radio not,
here I come!

Knock, knock.
Who's there?
Tyrone.
Tyrone who?
Tyrone shoelaces!

Knock, knock.
Who's there?
Anita.
Anita who?
Anita borrow
a pencil!

Knock, knock.
Who's there?
Robin.
Robin who?
Robin you!
Now give me
all your money!!

Knock, knock.
Who's there?
Andrew.
Andrew who?
Andrew a picture!

Knock, knock.
Who's there?
Annie.
Annie who?
Annie body
going to open
this door!

Knock, knock.
Who's there?
Wayne.
Wayne who?
Wayne drops
are falling on
my head.

Knock, knock.
Who's there?
Annie.
Annie who?
Annie thing
you can do I
can do better!

Knock, knock.
Who's there?
Barbara.
Barbara who?
Barbara black
sheep, have
you any wool?

Knock, knock.
Who's there?
Ben.
Ben who?
Ben knocking
for 20 minutes
already!

Knock, knock.
Who's there?
Nobel
Nobel who?
No bell, that's
why I knocked!

Knock, knock.
Who's there?
Justin.
Justin who?
Justin the
neighborhood
and thought
I'd stop by.

52

Knock, knock.
Who's there?
Gorilla.
Gorilla who?
Gorilla me a
cheese sandwich!

Knock, knock.
Who's there?
Ken.
Ken who?
Ken I come in?
It's freezing
out here!

Knock, knock.
Who's there?
Yukon.
Yukon. who?
Yukon say
that again!

Knock, knock.
Who's there?
Tank.
Tank who?
You're welcome!

Knock, knock.
Who's there?
Kent.
Kent who?
Kent you tell
who I am by
my voice?

Knock, knock.
Who's there?
Lena.
Lena who?
Lena little closer
and I'll tell you!

Knock, knock.
Who's there?
Alpaca.
Alpaca who?
Alpaca the
trunk, you pack
the suitcase!

Knock, knock.
Who's there?
Luke.
Luke who?
Luke through
the keyhole
to see!

53

Knock, knock.
Who's there?
Wooden shoe.
Wooden shoe who?
Wooden shoe
like to hear
another joke?

Knock, knock.
Who's there?
Mikey.
Mikey who?
Mikey doesn't
fit in the keyhole!

Knock, knock.
Who's there?
The interrupting cow.
The interrupting
cow wh....
MOO!

Knock, knock.
Who's there?
Otto.
Otto who?
Otto know what's
taking you so long!

Knock, knock.
Who's there?
Ima.
Ima who?
Ima gonna
tickle you.

Knock, knock.
Who's there?
Robin.
Robin who?
Robin your house!

Knock, knock.
Who's there?
Sherlock.
Sherlock who?
Sherlock your
door shut tight.

Knock, knock.
Who's there?
Rough.
Rough who?
Rough, rough, rough!
It's your dog!

Knock, knock.
Who's there?
Candice.
Candice who?
Candice joke possibly
get any worse?

Knock knock.
Who's there?
Butter.
Butter, who?
I butter not tell you.

Knock, knock.
Who's there?
Claire.
Claire who?
Claire the way;
I'm coming in!

Knock, knock.
Who's there?
Poop Poop who?
HAHAA made
you say poo-poo!

Knock, knock.
Who's there?
Doris.
Doris who?
Doris locked.
Open up, please!

Knock, knock.
Who's there?
Dwayne.
Dwayne who?
Dwayne the
bathtub —
I'm drowning!

Knock, knock.
Who's there?
Cow-go.
Cow-go who?
No, Cow go MOO!

Knock, knock.
Who's there?
Frank.
Frank who?
Frank you for
being my friend.

55

Knock, knock.
Who's there?
Ya.
Ya, who?
I'm excited to
see you too!

Knock, knock.
Who's there?
Howard.
Howard who?
Howard I know?

Knock, knock.
Who's there?
Water.
Water who?
Water you doing
in my house?

Knock, knock
Who's there?
Goat.
Goat who?
Goat the door
and find out.

Knock, knock.
Who's there?
Isabel.
Isabel who?
Isabel working?
I had to knock.

Knock, knock
Who's there?
Almat.
Almat who?
Almat going
to tell you!

56

Science

Jokes

How did Benjamin Franklin
feel when he discovered
electricity?

Shocked!

Why can't you
trust atoms?

Because they make
up everything.

How do you stop
an astronaut's baby
from crying?

You rocket!

Who can solve the
problem best,
a mathematician
or a chemist?

Chemist, because all
solutions are there
with them handy.

I'm reading a book
about anti-gravity.

It's impossible
to put down.

Molecule 1: I just lost
an electron.
Molecule 2: Are you sure?
Molecule 1: I'm positive.

When Magnesium and
Oxygen started dating
I was like, "O MG!"

Eye doctors are the
most ill-treated doctors.
Do you know why?
Because they are hardly
seen by the patients.

What kind of ghosts
haunt chemistry labs?

Methylated Spirits!

Did you hear about the restaurant on the moon?

Great food but no atmosphere.

How does a scientist freshen her breath?

With experi-mints!

What did the limestone say to the Geologist?

Don't take me for granite!

Why didn't the sun go to college?

Because it already had a million degrees!

A neutron walked into a bar and asked, "How much for a drink?" The bartender replied, "For you, no charge."

A photon walks into a hotel. The desk clerk says, "Welcome to our hotel. Can we help you with your luggage?" The photon says, "No thanks, I'm traveling light."

The rotation of the earth really makes my day.

How do you cut the sea in half?

With a see saw!

What do planets like to read?

Comet books!

I heard today that the molecular formula for water is no longer H_2O...... it's now HIJKLMNO

I would make another chemistry joke, but they ARGON.

The love between blood cells is a failure because all their efforts go in vein.

I'd tell you a chemistry joke... But I know I wouldn't get a reaction.

Where do flowers like to shop in Spring?

Bloomingdale's.

How do trees get on the internet?

They log in!

Anyone know any jokes about sodium?

Na

Why couldn't the astronaut book a room on the moon?

It was full!

Did you hear oxygen went on a date with potassium?

It went OK.

What do you do with a sick scientist?

Well if you can't helium and you can't curium then you might as well barium.

What type of bears dissolve in water?

Polar bears.

Why did the germ
cross the microscope?

To get to the
other slide!

Rock says to Lava,
"You're hot!"
Lava says to Rock,
"You rock."

Proton says
to Electron,
"I am sick of
your negativity."

Everybody should
have a friend who's
a Chemist. Why?

Because they have
all the solutions.

What is a cation afraid of?

A dogion.

What kind of hair
do oceans have?

Wavy!

What do scientists
use to freshen
their breath?

Experi-mints!

Name the favorite
dog of Charles Darwin?

A lab.

What weapon can
you make from the
chemicals Potassium,
Nickel and Iron?

KNiFe.

What's the difference
between a dog and a
marine biologist?

One wags a tail and
the other tags a whale.

What type of music do
planets dance to?

Nep-tunes!

How can you spot a
Chemist in the bathroom?

They wash their hands
before using the toilet.

What does Earth
say to tease the
other planets?

"You guys have no life."

If the Silver Surfer
and Iron Man team up,
they'd be alloys.

Organic chemistry is
difficult. Those who
study it have alkynes
of trouble.

Why didn't the
firefly get good
grades in school?

He wasn't very bright!

What did the
thermometer say to the
graduated cylinder?

At least I have a degree!

Did you hear the one
about the astronaut
who stepped in gum?

All the good chemistry
jokes Argon?

I don't Zinc so.

Satellite photos are
the Earth's selfies!

He got stuck in Orbit.

What did Sodium
say to Chlorine?

I've got my ion you!

Mountains are
not just funny,
they're hill areas.

What's a
Chemist's favorite
morning drink?

CoFe2

What's worse than
finding a worm in
your apple?

Finding half a worm!

Research is a thing
you do when you
don't know what
you are doing!

In 1905, Albert
Einstein published a
theory about space.
And it was about time.

What would you
call a re-make of
the film TRON?

Neutron (New-TRON).

What do you do with
a dead chemists?

Barium.

What goes zzub, zubb?

A bee flying backwards!

What do chemists
call a benzene ring
with iron atoms replacing
the carbon atoms?

A ferrous wheel.

What do clouds do when
they become rich?

They make it rain!

Want to hear a
Potassium joke?

K.

How do we know
that Saturn was
marries many times?

Because she has
many rings!

What is the name
of the first electricity
detective?

Sherlock Ohms.

How much room does
a fungus need to grow?

As mushroom as possible.

Why do tigers
have stripes?

So they don't
get spotted.

What did Neil Armstrong
do after he stepped on
Buzz Aldrin's toe?

He Apollo-gized.

What do you call
someone who steals
energy?

A Joule thief!

What's the first
thing you should
learn in chemistry?

Never lick
the spoon.

What was the
first animal to go
into space?

The cow that jumped
over the moon!

What did the
beach say when the
tide came in? ...

Long time no sea.

Why was the
ant so confused?

Because all his
uncles were "ants!"

What is the
chemical formula
for banana?

BaNa2

What would you call
a funny element?

He he he
(helium helium helium)

What has a bed that
you can't sleep in?

A river!

What did the nuclear
physicist have for lunch?

Fission Chips.

What is the most
egoist creature
living in the sea?

The "shelfish".

Biology is the only
science in which
multiplication is the
same thing as division.

Why is electricity
so dangerous?

It doesn't
conduct itself.

What do you call a snake that is 3.14 meters long?

A Pi-thon.

What do computers like to eat?

Chips

Math

Jokes

What area of a room
is the warmest?

The corner. It is always
about 90 degrees!

Why isn't the nose
12 inches long?

Because then it
would be a foot.

Teacher: If you got
$20 from 5 people,
what do you get?

Student: A new bike!

Why was 6
scared of 7?

Because 7 8 9
(seven ate nine).

Why couldn't the
math student get
any attention?

He didn't count!

What did one math
book say to the other?

I've got so many
problems.

Why was the math
student so bad at
decimals?

She couldn't
get the point!

Teacher: If I had 6
apples in one hand and
7 oranges in the other,
what would I have?

Student: Big hands!

Why did the student
get upset when his teacher
called him average?

It was a mean thing to say!

Last night I dreamt
that I was weightless.
I was like 0mg.

What do mathematicians
eat on Halloween?

Pumpkin Pi.

Why should you
never mention the
number 288?

Because it's "two" gross
(two ate ate).

Who invented
the fractions?

Henry the Eighth!

What kind of tree could
a math teacher climb?

Geometry.

What is a polygon?

A dead parrot!

What do you get
if you cross a math
teacher and a clock?

Arithma-ticks!

Why did the girl
wear glasses during
math class?

Because it improves
di-vison.

Why couldn't the
angle get a loan?

Its parents
wouldn't cosine.

Why do plants
hate math?

Because it gives
them square roots.

What do butterflies
study at school?

Mothematics!

I saw my math
teacher with a piece of
graph paper yesterday.

I think he must be
plotting something.

What was T. rex's
favorite number?

Eight (ate).

Have you heard the
latest statistics joke?

Probably.

Why do teenagers travel
in groups of three?

Because they can't even.

What's black, white
and horrible?

A math test!

Why was the "="
sign so humble?

He knew he wasn't ">"
or "<" anyone else.

I saw Pi fighting
with the square
root of two the
other day.

I told them to stop
being so irrational.

Today I saw the number
6 playing with the square
root of -1. I thought to
myself, "How cute-he
has an imaginary friend."

How many monsters
are good at math?

None, unless you
Count Dracula.

Why did the two
4's skip lunch?

They already 8 (ate).

Why couldn't the
number four get
through the door?

Because it was
too square.

What did the rectangle
say to the circle?

You are totally
pointless.

The farmer only
counted 297 cows in
the field... But when
he rounded them up,
he had 300!

What math test are
bullies great at?

Pounding numbers.

Did you know that
6 out of 5 people have
difficulty with fractions?

What do you call
a man who spent all
summer at the beach?

A tangent.

Perpenticular lines
get into heaven only
because they meet...
the right angels!

Why was 8 afraid of 2?

Because 288.

Why did the number
4 eat 2 turnips?

Because 2 is the
square root of 4.

Teacher: What are parallel lines?

Student: They are vegetarians. They never meat.

What did the calculator say to the math student?

You can count on me.

Why did the student sit on the floor to do her multiplication problems?

The teacher told her not to use tables!

What do you call two dudes who bond over math?

Algebros!

What is the best way to find a math tutor?

Place an add!

Teacher: What's 2 and 2?
Student: 4
Teacher: That's good.
Student: Good? That's perfect!

What do baby parabolas drink?

Quadratic formula.

Where do math teachers go on vacation?

To Times Square!

What is 67 + 35 + 99 + 136 + 84?

A headache.

What did Al Gore
play on his guitar?

An algorithm!

I went into math class
today and said to my
teacher, "To show you
how well I understand
fractions, I've only
done half of my
homework."

Why should you never
get in an argument
with an obtuse triangle?

Because they're
never right!

How many sides does
a circle have?

Two - the inside
and the outside.

Which snakes are
good at math?

Adders.

Why did the
Romans think algebra
was so easy?

They knew X
was always 10!

What kind of meals
do math teachers eat?

Square meals.

Knock, knock
Who's there?
Algy.
Algy who?
Algy-bra.

Why was the geometry
lecture so long?

The professor kept
going off on a tangent!

What is a
mathematician's
favorite season?

Sum-mer.

How does a
mathematician
plow fields?

With a pro-tractor.

What did one algebra
book say to the other?

Don't bother me,
I've got my own problems.

Do you know
a statistics joke?

Probably, but it's mean!

What did the tree
say to the math teacher?

Gee-I'm-a-tree!
(Geometry)

What is a
mathematician's
favorite dessert?

Pi.

What has eight
legs and eight eyes?

Eight pirates!

Why didn't the
quarter roll down the
hill with the nickel?

Because it had
more cents.

Did you hear
about the constipated
mathematician?

He worked it
out with a pencil.

Why was the fraction
apprehensive about
marrying the decimal?

Because he would
have to convert.

How do you make
seven an even number?

By taking out the "s".

Why is your nose in
the middle of your face?

Because it is the
scenter! (center)

Which knight helped
King Arthur build his
round table?

Sir Cumference!

Why wasn't the
geometry teacher
at school?

Because she sprained
her angle!!

What U.S. state
has the most maths
teachers?

Mathachussets.

Which tables do you
not have to learn?

Dinner tables.

What do you call
dudes who love math?

Alge-bros.

What did the kid
say to his math?

You know some day,
you will have to solve
your own problems!

Why dont people
put the numbers 2,3,
and 0 together?

Because they are
two turdy (two thirty)!

A circle is just
a round straight
line with a hole
in the middle.

What do you call
numbera that can't
stay still?

Roamin' numerals.

What did the circle
say to the tangent line?

"Stop touching me!"

Why should you
never talk to Pi?

Because she'll go on
and on and on forever.

What are ten things
you can always count on?

Your fingers!

Matt had 60 cookies.
He ate 30 of them.
What does he have now?

A tummy ache.

I'll do algebra,
I'll do trig.
I'll even do statistics.
But graphing is where
I draw the line!

What's the best
way to flirt with
a math teacher?

Use acute angle.

Why did the math
book get poor grades?

It never did
it's own work.

Miscellaneous Jokes

A burger walks intoa bar. Barman says, "Sorry, we don't serve food in here."

Dad, can you put my shoes on?

No, I don't think they'll fit me.

I'll call you later. Don't call me later, call me dad.

The skeleton couldn't keep anything tidy because of his lazy bones.

I don't play soccer because I enjoy the sport. I'm just doing it for kicks.

"This is your captain speaking, AND THIS IS YOUR CAPTAIN SHOUTING."

This egg is bad! Don't blame me, I only laid the table!

I told my doctor that I broke my arm in two places. He told me to stop going to those places.

That skeleton sure brought his appetite to the picnic—and also some spare ribs.

What is a plumber's favorite vegetable?

A leek.

If you take your watch to be fixed, make sure you don't pay up front. Wait until the time is right.

Patient: "Doctor, I get heartburn every time I eat birthday cake."

Doctor: "Next time, take off the candles."

Sister: What are you giving Mom and Dad for Christmas?
Brother: A list of everything I want!

Forget about the past, you can't change it.
Forget about the future, you can't predict it.
Forget about the present, I didn't get you one.

What vegetable do you get when a large animal walks through your garden?

Squash!

A police recruit was asked during the exam, "What would you do if you had to arrest your own mother?"

He said, "Call for backup."

Fiona asks her daddy, "Dad, can you write with your eyes closed?"
"I believe I could, child, if I tried."
"Excellent, do you think you would like to try it on my school report?"

Bill Gates farted in an Apple store. He later commented, "Well it's hardly my fault they don't have any Windows..."

A boy comes home and proudly announces
to his parents, "Mom, dad, the teacher
asked the class a question today and I
was the only one who knew the right answer!"

The parents are very happy and ask, "That's
amazing Lenny! And what was the question?"

Sticking out his chest, the boys says,
"Who farted?"

How do the fish
get to school?

By octobus!

What do you call
fishing when you don't
catch any fish?

Drowning worms!

fi yuo cna raed tihs
whit no porlbem, yuo
aer smrat. Shaer ti
whit yuor fienrds.

What do you call
a rabbit with fleas?

Bugs Bunny!

Why was the knight
running around, yelling
for a tin opener?

There was a bee in
his suit of armor!

How does a celebrity
stay cool?

By keeping close
to his fans.

Snake's last words?

"Oh drat, I bit
my tongue!"

What's brown, hairy
and wears sunglasses?

A coconut on vacation!

What pet makes the
loudest noise?

A trum-pet!

What did the alien
ask the garden?

Take me to your weeder.

Why do hens lay eggs?

Because if they
were throwing them,
they'd break!

A skeleton made a bet,
claiming he's going to
fart really loud in a
crowded place. But
he didn't in the end.
He just didn't have
the guts!

What do you call a
tyrannosaurus that
talks and talks
and talks?

A dinobore!

Why is 2+2=5 like
your left foot?

It's not right.

What did the tie
say to the hat?

You go on ahead and
I'll hang around!

Why couldn't the
flower ride his bike?

Because he lost
his petals!

When do you stop
at green and go full
speed at red?

When you're enjoying
a watermelon!

Mother's advice:
Stop whining. Look what
the couch has to endure.
It has to stand every
fart and silently.

What do you do if a teacher
rolls her eyes at you?

Pick them up and roll
them back to her!

What school subject
is the fruitiest?

History because
it is full of dates!

Teacher: Didn't I tell
you to stand at the
end of the line?

Student: I tried but
there was someone
already there!

What did the blanket
say to the bed?

Got you covered!

We have scales!

How do fish always
know how much they
weigh?

Because they have
their own scales.

What do you get
when you cross a vampire
and a teacher?

Lots of blood tests!

What is invisible and
smells of worms?

A bird's fart.

What do get when
you cross one principal
with another principal?

I wouldn't do it,
principals don't like
to be crossed!

What is black and white
and red all over?

A zebra with
a sunburn.

Why did the boy
throw a glass of water
out the window?

He wanted to
see a waterfall.

What do you call a
crushed angle?

A rec-tangle.

Teacher: Okay class,
when I ask you a
question, I want you
all to answer me
at once. How much
is six times 3?

Class: "At once!"

That awkward moment
when you make a false
excuse to go out of
the room to fart, but
when you come back in,
you realize you carried
the smell back with you.

That awkward moment
when your shoe makes
the wrong sound on the
floor and you know there's
no way to persuade anyone
you haven't just farted.

Did you hear the joke
about the germ?

Never mind. I don't want
to spread it around.

How can you open
a banana?

With a mon-key!

Why are school cafeteria
workers cruel?

Because they batter
fish, beat eggs, and
whip cream.

Why does Little
Johnny always tiptoe
past the medicine box?

He's afraid what
would happen if he woke
up the sleeping pills.

Why did the teacher
draw on the window?

Because he wanted his
lesson to be very clear!

Don't you hate it when you fart under your blanket, lift your foot to air it out but instead you unintentionally lift the other end of the blanket and get the full load in your face?

Teacher: "You got a zero in the last exam."
Roger: "I don't think I deserve a zero!"
Teacher: "Neither do I. But I can't go any lower than that."

What flies around the kindergarten room at night?

The alpha-BAT.

Pamela says on her 16th birthday, "Daddy, don't you think I'm old enough to get my drivers' licence?"

Father replies, "You – yes. Our car – no."

Where do boats go when they are sick?

To the doc(k).

What do you call a snowman with a six pack?

An abdominal snowman.

What did the ghost teacher say to his class?

How do you start a communication with a fish?

You drop him a line!

"Look at the board and I'll go through it again!"

What did the mayonnaise say to the bread?

Close the door, I'm dressing.

What's taken before you get it?

Your picture.

Little Boy: Mummy, when was I born?
Mummy: 20th of April.
Little Boy: Wow, what a coincidence. It is the exact date when I have my birthday.

What object is king of the classroom?

The ruler!

Why did the Cyclops close his school?

Because he only had one pupil.

What runs around a farm but doesn't move?

A fence.

What do you call leftover aliens?

Extra Terrestrials.

Why does a woodpecker have a beak?

So as not to smash his head against the tree.

How come you didn't get me a present for my birthday?

Well, you did tell me to surprise you.

Why did the barber win the race?

Because he took a short cut.

What did the student say
after the teacher said,
"Order students, order?"

"Can I have fries and a burger?"

Chair

Why did the new boy steal
a chair from the classroom?

Because the teacher told
him to take a seat.

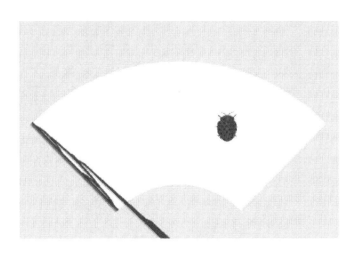

What did the bug say when
it hit the windshield?

I don't have the guts
to do that again.

Where do New York City kids
learn their multiplication tables?

Times Square.

Riddles

Here is a nice mixture of riddles for all ages and abilities. These puzzles will test and tease your brain!

** Warning **

The answers may have
a LOL effect on you!!

You will find the answers at the end
of this section.

Enjoy!

1. What gets wetter
the more it dries?

2. What has teeth
but can't eat?

3. I have no feet,
no hands, no wings,
I can climb to the sky.
What am I?

4. Cloud is my mother.
Wind is my father.
I come down but never go up.
What am I?

5. You shoot me but I don't die.
You hang me but I don't die.
But if you burn me, I die.
What am I?

6. I begin your sentence.
What am I?

7. You hold my tail while
I fish for you.
What am I?

8. I touch the earth, I touch the sky.
But if I touch you, you may die.
What am I?

9. What belongs to you but
others use more?

10. I have no wings yet I can fly.
I have no eye yet I can cry.
What am I?

11. What word when read from
left to right is a ruler but when
read from right to left is a servant?

12. What goes through a door but
never goes in and never comes out?

13. What goes up when the
rain come down?

14. What cup can't hold water?

15. The more you take, the more
you leave behind. What am I?

16. What ancient invention lets you look right through the wall?

17. What occurs once in a minute, twice in a moment and never in one thousand years?

18. What begins with T, ends with T and has T in it?

19. Which month has 28 days?

20. A bridge can only hold two people. If three people cross it at the same time, it will collapse. One night, a king and his son cross the bridge.
It collapses.
Why?

21. A woman has seven daughters and each daughter has a brother. How many children does the woman have all together?

22. I can run but I don't know how to walk.
Who am I?

23. What is lighter than a feather,
but still you can't lift it?

24. I am loved by vehicles and they take
me inside. But people hate me and throw
me out. Who am I?

25. What type of cheese is made
backwards?

26. Imagine you're in a room that is
filling with water. There are no windows
or doors. How do you get out?

27. What has hands but doesn't clap?

28. If a red house is made of red bricks,
and a yellow house is made of yellow
bricks, what is a greenhouse made of?

29. What has a neck but no head?

30. What five-letter word becomes
shorter when you add two letters to it?

31. You can you serve it, but never eat it? What is it?

32. What goes up and down but never moves?

33. I'm tall when I'm young, and I'm short when I'm old, what am I?

34. How do you make the number one disappear?

35. Which letter of the alphabet has the most water?

36. What starts with a P, ends with an E and has thousands of letters?

37. Which weighs more, a pound of feathers or a pound of bricks?

38. What word is spelled wrong in every dictionary?

39. You draw a line. Without touching it, how do you make it a longer line?

40. What needs an answer but doesn't ask a question?

41. If you took two apples from three apples how many apples would you have?

42. What has to be broken before you can use it?

43. What is as light as a feather but even the strongest man in the world can't hold it for long?

44. Why would a man living in New York not be buried in Chicago?

45. What do the numbers 11, 69 and 88 all have in common?

46. What is so fragile that saying its name breaks it?

47. What gets bigger and bigger the more you take away from it?

48. Three men were in a boat.
It capsized, but only two got
their hair wet. Why?

49. How many seconds
are there in a year?

50. If a brother, his sister,
his mom, his dad and their dog
weren't under an umbrella,
why didn't they get wet?

51. What can be as big as an
elephant but weigh nothing?

52. After a train crashed,
every single person died.
Who survived?

53. If I have it, I don't share it.
If I share it, I don't have it.
What is it?

54. The more you have of it,
the less you see.
What is it?

55. Where does Friday come
before Thursday?

56. What is the difference between
a jeweler and a jailer?

57. Name four days of the week that
start with the letter "T."

58. What has four eyes but can't see?

59. If it takes one man three days to
dig a hole, how long does it take two men
to dig half a hole?

60. Bobby throws a ball as hard as he can.
It comes back to him, even though nothing
and nobody touches it.
How?

61. A word I know, six letters it contains,
remove one letter and 12 remains, what is it?

62. What do you throw out when
you want to use it, but take in
when you don't want to use it?

63. If an electric train is travelling south, which way is the smoke going?

64. What answer can you never answer yes to?

65. If you were in a race and passed the person in 2nd place, what place would you be in?

66. They come out at night without being called, and are lost in the day without being stolen. What are they?

67. What does this mean?
I RIGHT I

68. What is always in front of you but can't be seen?

69. I saw a boat full of people, yet there wasn't a single person on the boat. How?

70. What is next in this sequence?
JFMAMJJASON . . .

71. Where can you find cities, towns, shops, and streets but no people?

72. How many bricks does it take to complete a building made from bricks?

73. How much dirt is in a hole 5 feet wide and 4 feet deep?

74. Why do lions eat raw meat?

75. A boy fell off a 20-foot ladder but did not get hurt. Why not?

76. What's black and white and blue?

77. If two's company and three's a crowd, what are four and five?

78. What bird can
lift the most?

79. What do lazy
dogs do for fun?

80. What two keys
can't open any door?

Answer to the Riddles

1. A towel
2. A comb
3. Smoke
4. Rain
5. A picture
6. Capital
7. Net
8. Lightning
9. Your name
10. Cloud
11. God
12. A keyhole
13. Umbrella
14. A cupcake
15. Footsteps
16. Windows
17. The letter M
18. Teapot

19. All of them
20. Replace night
    with knight
21. She has eight
    children!
22. Water
23. Air
24. Gas
25. Edam
26. Stop imagining!
27. A clock
28. Glass, all
    greenhouses are
    made of glass.
29. A bottle
30. Short
31. A tennis ball
32. The temperature

33. A candle
34. Add the letter 'G' and it's Gone
35. The C
36. Post office
37. Neither. They both weigh one pound.
38. Wrong
39. Draw a short line next to it and now it's the longer line
40. A telephone
41. Two apples – the two that you took
42. An egg
43. His breath
44. Because he is still living
45. The read the same right side up and upside down
46. Silence
47. A hole
48. One was bald
49. Twelve. January 2nd, February 2nd, March 2nd...
50. It wasn't raining
51. Its shadow
52. All of the couples
53. A secret
54. Darkness
55. In the dictionary
56. A jeweler sells watches. A jailer watches cells
57. Tuesday, Thursday, today, and tomorrow
58. Mississippi
59. You can't dig half a hole!
60. He throws it straight up
61. Dozens
62. An anchor
63. There is no smoke; it is an electric train!
64. Are you asleep yet?
65. 2nd
66. Stars
67. Right between the eyes
68. The future
69. They were all married
70. The letter "D." The sequence contains the first letter of each month
71. A map
72. One – the last one
73. None
74. Because they never learned to cook
75. He fell off the bottom step
76. A sad zebra
77. Nine
78. A crane
79. Chase parked cars
80. A monkey and a donkey

Made in the USA
San Bernardino, CA
07 December 2019